# STOCKHOLM
## THE CITY AT A GLANCE

G000134345

### Royal Palace
Designed by Nicodemus Tessin, the
608-room palace was completed
Royal Family now resides in the Drottningholm
and Haga Palaces, so you can visit the state
quarters and three fascinating museums.
*Slottsbacken 1, T 402 6130*

### Riksdagshuset
Little Helgeandsholmen (Isle of the Holy
Spirit) is almost completely taken up by the
Swedish Parliament. The modern section,
added in the 1970s, is a great example of
marrying contemporary styles with old.
*Riksgatan 3, T 786 4019*

### Stadshuset
Designed by Ragnar Östberg and inaugurated
in 1923, City Hall is Stockholm's most iconic
building. Climb the 106m tower (summer only)
or book a guided tour to see the Blue Hall,
which hosts the annual Nobel Prize banquet.
*Hantverkargatan 1, T 5082 9000*

### Västerbron
Many locals state that this 1935 bridge is
their favourite vantage point in the city.
A 300m walk to its apex will reward you with
spectacular views across the archipelago.

### Central Station
The city's main railway hub, Central Station
has a vast waiting hall and is the place from
which to catch the Arlanda Express – the
super-efficient 20-minute ride to the airport.
*Klarabergsviadukten*

### Hötorgsskraporna
These five aligned 72m curtain-walled
modernist blocks built between 1952 and
1966 stand out on Stockholm's low skyline.
*Sveavägen*

# INTRODUCTION
## THE CHANGING FACE OF THE URBAN SCENE

Stockholm conjures up an image of a clean, ordered place full of fashionable blondes. Yet, while it will always retain a touch of Nordic cool, the Swedish capital is morphing into a multicultural city. Almost 30 per cent of residents have a foreign background and more than 180 nationalities are represented in the metropolitan area. As a result, its cultural offerings are far richer than a decade ago, and the focus is expanding from the central areas – although well-groomed Östermalm and boho-chic Södermalm remain as interesting as ever, having acquired a more cosmopolitan feel.

The capital has also altered stylistically. In the early noughties, the city's reputation for sleek minimalism made it a pilgrimage site for the design conscious, but today it has achieved a maturity which challenges the notion that Stockholm and its inhabitants are 'only' ravishingly beautiful. The ubiquitous white tabletops, clean seating areas and tea-light ambience have been updated, and commercial interiors have developed individual, experimental and altogether more fun undertones. The locals, with their superb English, zest for life and love of travelling, have taken all the global influences to heart. Yet amid their enthusiasm is a strong sense of self-awareness. Stockholmers have an incredible ability to never take things too far. Whether it's in design, architecture, fashion or cuisine, Swedes always seem to achieve the ideal balance. They've even got the perfect word for it, *lagom*, which means 'just right'.

# ESSENTIAL INFO

## FACTS, FIGURES AND USEFUL ADDRESSES

### TOURIST OFFICE
*Vasagatan 14*
*T 5082 8508*
*www.visitstockholm.com*

### TRANSPORT
**Car hire**
Avis
*T 010 494 8050*
**Metro**
*T 600 1000*
*www.sl.se/english*
Trains run from approximately 5am to 1am
**Taxis**
Taxi 020
*T 020 202 020*
Taxi Kurir
*T 300 000*
Taxi Stockholm
*T 150 000*
Avoid unofficial cabs, especially at Arlanda

### EMERGENCY SERVICES
**Emergencies**
*T 112*
**Police (non-emergency)**
*T 114 14*
**24-hour pharmacy**
Apotek CW Scheele
*Klarabergsgatan 64*
*T 077 145 0450*
*www.apoteket.se*

### EMBASSIES
**British Embassy**
*Skarpögatan 6-8*
*T 671 3000*
*www.ukinsweden.fco.gov.uk*
**US Embassy**
*Dag Hammarskjölds Väg 31*
*T 783 5300*
*stockholm.usembassy.gov*

### POSTAL SERVICES
**Post office**
Hemköp
*Mäster Samuelsgatan 57*
*T 723 6530*
**Shipping**
UPS
*T 411 7010*

### BOOKS
**City of My Dreams** by Per Anders
Fogelström (Penfield Press)
**The Complete Guide to Architecture
in Stockholm** by Olof Hultin, Bengt Oh
Johansson, Johan Märtelius and Rasmus
Wærn (Arkitektur Förlag)
**The Girl with the Dragon Tattoo**
by Stieg Larsson (MacLehose Press)

### WEBSITES
**Design**
*www.svenskform.se*
**Newspaper**
*www.thelocal.se*

### EVENTS
**Market**
*www.market-art.se*
**Stockholm Furniture Fair**
*www.stockholmfurniturefair.se*

### COST OF LIVING
**Taxi from Arlanda Airport to city centre**
SEK520
**Cappuccino**
SEK25
**Packet of cigarettes**
SEK50
**Daily newspaper**
SEK20
**Bottle of champagne**
SEK700

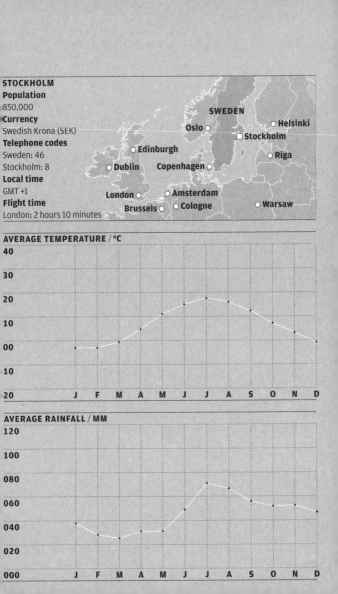

**STOCKHOLM**
**Population**
850,000
**Currency**
Swedish Krona (SEK)
**Telephone codes**
Sweden: 46
Stockholm: 8
**Local time**
GMT +1
**Flight time**
London: 2 hours 10 minutes

SWEDEN

Oslo ○   ○ Helsinki
□ Stockholm

○ Edinburgh   ○ Riga

○ Dublin   Copenhagen ○

London ○   ○ Amsterdam

Brussels ○   ○ Cologne   ○ Warsaw

**AVERAGE TEMPERATURE / °C**

| | J | F | M | A | M | J | J | A | S | O | N | D |

40
30
20
10
00
10
20

**AVERAGE RAINFALL / MM**

120
100
080
060
040
020
000

| | J | F | M | A | M | J | J | A | S | O | N | D |

# NEIGHBOURHOODS

## THE AREAS YOU NEED TO KNOW AND WHY

To help you navigate the city, we've chosen the most interesting districts (see below and the map inside the back cover) and colour-coded our featured venues, according to their location; those venues that are outside these areas are not coloured.

### ÖSTERMALM

Encompassing Sweden's most sought-after properties, manicured boulevards and chic shopping streets, Östermalm is where to check out which labels are in and which are 'so last year'. A mix of yummy mummies, the media set and plenty of old money, its happy residents rarely go anywhere else.

### SKEPPSHOLMEN

Otherwise known as Museum Island, this tiny enclave was once heavily littered with military buildings; today it is to all intents and purposes made up of the Svensk Form (Svensksundsvägen 13, T 463 3130) design foundation, Moderna Museet (see p009) and Arkitekturmuseet (see p064). All three are well worth visiting.

### NORRMALM

Bustling, central Norrmalm is the capital's business hub. Filled with offices, coffee chains and lunch spots, it's not exactly quaint, but when it contains Stockholm's largest department store, NK (Hamngatan 18-22, T 762 8000) – the equivalent of Selfridges – then who needs cute?

### SÖDERMALM

Until 10 years ago, parts of Södermalm were considered too dangerous to venture into at night (in Swedish terms at least), but today it is a creative, boho part of town that tells a different story, full of beatnik cafés and bars (see p041), yoga studios and cool stores and boutiques (see p084).

### VASASTADEN

This mainly residential district attracts families who are looking for more space but still want the benefits of inner-city life. Several bars and restaurants have sprung up to give the place an increasingly hip vibe, but for the most part it is known for local eateries and organic delis.

### GAMLA STAN

Packed full of character and tourists, the Old Town is a maze of cobbled streets and terracotta-coloured buildings, containing dining spots, bars and gift shops. Veer off the main strip, Västerlanggatan, to find some charming antiques shops, adorable cafés and outstanding restaurants, including Frantzén/Lindeberg (see p058).

### KUNGSHOLMEN

An up-and-coming residential area, this island provides for the creatives pushed out of Östermalm by rocketing rents. Huge houses have been converted into loft-living spaces, with a few cosy bistros (see p054) and small galleries springing up on these otherwise deserted streets.

### DJURGÅRDEN

Lush, green Djurgården (see p033) is the city's oasis. The park also contains the zoo, a funfair and several museums, and manages to do so in the least tacky way possible. The path along the water, shaded by trees, is definitely up there with the best jogging routes in the world.

# LANDMARKS

## THE SHAPE OF THE CITY SKYLINE

Alongside the canvases and photographs lining the walls of the
Moderna Museet (Skeppsholmen, T 5195 5289), a striking minimal
late-1990s building designed by Rafael Moneo in collaboration
with architects White, are large rectangular windows that reveal
breathtaking snapshots of Stockholm's harbour. In other words,
for the Swedes, a landscape view is just as beautiful as any work
of art. Then again, given that the city is built on 14 islands and a
series of 30,000 smaller ones in the archipelago beyond, it is not
surprising that it casts a pretty picture. Separated only by a short
walk over one of 57 bridges, each of the main islands has its own
character. Norrmalm has a buzzy, city-centre feel, whereas Gamla
Stan, just a stop away on the subway, is all picturesque cobbled
streets and cosy cafés. Östermalm, which is a dense residential
and shopping area, is very different from lush, green Djurgården
(see p033), but lies just a quick skip over Djurgårdsbron.

The cityscape is so dominated by the water that manmade
works tend to take second place, although Kaknästornet (see
p012), the telecoms building, can be seen from almost anywhere.
Newer structures, such as Stockholm Waterfront (overleaf) and
the Ericsson Globe (see p090), sit comfortably within the urban
panorama, and Kulturhuset (see p014), located slap bang in the
city centre, is perhaps the ideal landmark by which to navigate.
*For full addresses, see Resources.*

**Stockholm Waterfront**
Swedish architects White's SEK1.5bn
congress centre (pictured) and hotel
was accused of stealing the limelight
from the Stadshuset across the water
in 2011. The cantilevered upper volume
is shielded by 3,500 reflective stainless-
steel strips arranged to form an organic
shape that evokes the movement seen
on the surrounding flyovers and quays.
*Nils Ericsons Plan 4, T 5050 6000*

### Kaknästornet

Known as the central 'spider' in the web of Sweden's TV and radio networks, this imposing 155m-high steel and concrete structure bears little resemblance to an arachnid. Drawn up by architects Bengt Lindroos and Hans Borgström, it took four years to build and was inaugurated in 1967. Like so many 1960s buildings, the stark tower has divided city opinion over the years. Few residents, however, could argue that, on a fine day, the uninterrupted 60km views through the picture windows of the top-floor Skybar and the restaurant (which has undergone a refurb but doesn't quite make the grade in terms of dining) are anything but spectacular.

*Mörka Kroken 28-30, T 667 2105, www.kaknastornet.se*

**Wenner-Gren Centre**
Designed by Sune Lindström and Alf Bydén, and completed in 1962, this 74m high-rise is one of the tallest buildings in the country. The centre is named after the late Axel Wenner-Gren, a Swedish businessman who donated the funds for the project. It is composed of two main structures: the Helicon, a lower, circular building surrounding the tower (just visible in the background, above) that provides housing for visiting scientists, and the high-rise itself, the Pylon, which is home to a variety of Wenner-Gren foundations dedicated to the support of international scientific exchange.
*Sveavägen 164, T 736 9800, www.swgc.org*

## Kulturhuset

Peter Celsing's remarkable building is
a counterpoint to the commercialism of
Sergels Torg. Completed in 1974, it was no
simple task to incorporate the Kulturhuset
(Culture House) with the Riksbanken (Bank
of Sweden). Rather than try to unify two
such different functions, Celsing did the
opposite. The Bank is a heavy, introverted,
black granite cube, whereas the Culture
House was given a glass facade, resembling
an open, seven-storey shelf unit, so as to
be inviting and accessible, and showcase
the activities inside. The Stadsteatern
theatre company is based here, various
galleries exhibit, and in summer, the
rooftop hosts frequent concerts and film
screenings. It is also a regular location
for the monthly Lunch Beat dance craze
(noon to 1pm) that began in Stockholm
and has now caught on all over Europe.
*Sergels Torg, T 5083 1508,*
*www.kulturhuset.stockholm.se*

# HOTELS
## WHERE TO STAY AND WHICH ROOMS TO BOOK

Just a few years ago, Stockholm would have struggled to house the delegates for a large event or conference. This is no longer so, thanks to several hotels having opened, notably the mighty Clarion Sign (opposite), which has 558 rooms, and the smaller, 201-room Nobis (see p022). Both have been well received, but older institutions haven't fallen out of favour, and constant updates and impeccable service keep the established names on top. The opulent Grand (Södra Blasieholmshamnen 8, T 679 3500) refuses to rest on its laurels. It swallowed up the Burmanska Palace in 2006, and has been renovating ever since. The hip Berns (Näckströmsgatan 8, T 5663 2200) has also had a major overhaul; it may have matured since making its reputation through its celeb-filled nightclub, but there's no sign of this address' popularity or looks fading.

Although none of the new hotels could be defined as monolithic, save perhaps the Clarion (Ringvägen 98, T 462 1000), the boutique concept had been surprisingly overlooked till recently. Now, three properties are shaking up the scene – homely Ett Hem (see p018), happening Lydmar (see p020), whose bar alone is worth a visit, and bohemian Story (see p024). For classic art nouveau in a central location, the Esplanade (see p028) is a delight, but if you prefer to get away from it all, head to Gåshaga (see p026) or Skeppsholmen (see p030), where the sea views are unsurpassed. *For full addresses and room rates, see Resources.*

**Clarion Hotel Sign**

Designed by local architect Gert Wingårdh and opened in 2008, the Clarion is a glazed black beacon in the redeveloped Norra Bantorget district. One of the city's largest hotels, comprising 558 rooms, it's not for those seeking a cosy atmosphere. However, you will find Nordic furnishings and immaculate design. All of the rooms on the fourth floor have sofas or chairs by Norway Says, and the fifth floor is dedicated to Alvar Aalto. Rooms on floors six to 10, including the Superior Room 1005 (above), feature classics such as Arne Jacobsen's 'Egg' chair or Erik Jørgensen's 'EJ 250' sofa. Fans of Hans J Wegner's 'Ox' chair should book Suite 601. But the real treat is on the roof – the heated outdoor pool means you can swim even in winter. *Östra Järnvägsgatan 35, T 676 9800, www.clarionsign.com*

### Ett Hem

The name translates as 'a home', and indeed this boutique hotel offers a luxury that larger establishments cannot provide. The kitchen is open all hours and stocked with champagne and tasty morsels, and you can invite friends over for dinner. The lounge has a TV and board games, and there's also a bar, a decent library and a small spa/sauna. The 1910 brick building was designed in National Romantic style by Fredrik Dahlberg and is typical for the Lärkstaden district. It was converted from a private home in 2012, and designer Ilse Crawford has furnished it with antiques, vintage items, and art and photography from the owners' collection. The 12 rooms, such as Suite 1 (above and opposite), feature brass cocktail cabinets and tactile materials in natural tones, including cane, wood, leather and velvet.
*Sköldungagatan 2, T 200 590,*
*www.etthemstockholm.se*

**Lydmar Hotel**
An enviable location, offering views of Gamla Stan and the Royal Palace, and rooms that are unrivalled in their spaciousness, such as the X-Large (pictured), set Lydmar apart from the competition. Its restaurant is one of the most popular in the city, and has become a haunt of the beau monde. *Södra Blasieholmshamnen 2, T 223 160, www.lydmar.com*

### Nobis Hotel

Opened in 2010, this is probably the most sophisticated luxury hotel in town. Design trio Claesson Koivisto Rune have combined earthy colours, oak, Carrara marble and leather to create a space that doesn't make too much of a fuss about itself. The Gold Bar is a favourite for after-work drinks among locals and the downstairs restaurant Caina (T 614 1030) offers excellent Italian food; gastronomic director Stefano Catenacci is also chef de cuisine at Operakällaren (see p044). Some of the rooms, such as Deluxe 467 (above and opposite), overlook Berzelii Park, and the opulent Nobis Suite features late 19th-century stucco and wood panelling. *Norrmalmstorg 2-4, T 614 1000, www.nobishotel.se*

### Story Hotel

This bohemian 83-room boutique hotel is located in Stureplan, just a few steps from the shopping district of Östermalm. Opened in 2009, the hotel's mixture of downtown New York and Parisian salon has been a welcome addition to the local scene. The interior is a blend of industrial chic and opulence, and features exposed pipes, concrete floors and pillars, velvet furnishings and affordable art – signed limited-edition prints and photos, which are available to buy in the shop. On offer are 12 types of room, ranging from the Super Squeeze to the spacious Lily Dam Suite (opposite), with a bed as big as a plunge pool, so there's something for all. The happening bar and lounge (above) has DJs providing the mix from Wednesdays to Saturdays and there's a restaurant serving an Asian and European menu.
*Riddargatan 6, T 5450 3940,*
*www.storyhotels.com*

**Gåshaga Sealodge**
Half an hour by train or boat from the centre, Gåshaga has 13 rooms, each with a balcony and sea view. Its decor was inspired by a Newport summer house, as seen in the Yacht Club (pictured), a space that can be hired for events. The open fires and thick blankets may make you feel as if you're in a Ralph Lauren ad.
*Värdshusvägen 14-16, Lidingö,*
*T 601 3400, www.gashaga.nu*

## Hotel Esplanade

If you like your hotels to have character, this is the place for you. Photos in the breakfast room show the Esplanade in all its Jugendstil splendour, when it opened in 1910 as serviced apartments, and little has changed since. Gentle renovations have occurred over the years: the rooms have been given en-suite bathrooms; the period furniture has been re-upholstered, as seen in the upstairs lounge (above); and a small sauna has been added. However, the incredible art nouveau parquet flooring, wood panelling and fireplaces remain intact, such as in Room 14 (opposite). In short, what the place lacks in hi-tech gadgets and bathtub size, it more than makes up for in old-fashioned Scandinavian charm. *Strandvägen 7a, T 663 0740, www.hotelesplanade.se*

**Hotel Skeppsholmen**
Situated on one of the most picturesque
of Stockholm's islands, this 81-room hotel
is the perfect destination should you be
looking for a little peace. Housed in two
barrack buildings constructed in 1699, it
was designed by Claesson Koivisto Rune
in collaboration with Erséus Architects.
We recommend Room 254 (pictured).
*Gröna Gången 1, T 407 2350,*
*www.hotelskeppsholmen.se*

# 24 HOURS

## SEE THE BEST OF THE CITY IN JUST ONE DAY

Stockholm is a city of climatic opposites, as temperatures can fall to -15°C in the winter months and climb to a bright 25°C with almost 24 hours of daylight in summer, rendering a complete transformation. Equally notable are the urban contrasts to be navigated, from tranquil, bucolic landscape to bustling shopping district in the space of minutes. These extremes unite rather than divide the city, as Stockholmers embrace the milieu with gusto.

Swedish breakfast is another experience to sample. Pickled fish, strong cheese and crackerbread divide foreign tastes, but we rate the sourdough sandwich with liver paste and pickled cucumber at Albert & Jack's (see p034). Head to Östermalm for some of Europe's finest design showrooms, before lunch at KonstnärsBaren (see p045) or Matbaren (see p060). From there, it's a short walk to one of Scandinavia's foremost art collections at Moderna Museet (see p009). Or take a 15-minute cab ride out to the new upstart in town, the sprawling Artipelag (Artipelagstigen 1, Gustavsberg), designed by Johan Nyrén to blend in with a lovely setting among the pines above Baggen's Bay. After spending the evening at Lilla Baren (see p038), hit a nightclub, such as Marie Laveau (Hornsgatan 66, T 668 8500), where Sweden's best DJs play at weekends, or one of the kicking spots around Stureplan, or curl up with a hot chocolate and the old-world vibe at Kaffekoppen (Stortorget 20, T 203 170).
*For full addresses, see Resources.*

## 08.30 Djurgården

One of the 14 islands that constitute the City of Stockholm, Djurgården is a wooded park with shaded trails, grassy knolls and waterside pathways. A jog or stroll here, and a dip, is the ideal start to a summer's day. Within the park are a funfair, museums and restaurants; one of the cosiest is the canalside Djurgårdsbrunn (T 624 2200). An alternative option on winter weekends is to take a taxi to Solna for the brunch buffet at Haga Forum (T 334 844), which is loaded with herring, gravadlax, cheese, pancakes and more. The unbecoming exterior betrays the building's former life as a bus terminal, yet inside there's contemporary furniture and a roaring fire. Once you've refuelled, Haga Park lies nearby, and is a beautiful landscape of rolling snow-covered hills and 18th-century neoclassical pavilions (see p065).

### 10.00 Albert & Jack's

In a city without a deli culture, Albert
& Jack's is quite a find. Stockholmers
flock here for breakfast and lunch,
partaking of the freshly baked breads,
seasonal produce and exclusively blended
tea and coffee. Situated in a dock house
dating from 1640, the bakery nestles
among the cobbled alleyways of Gamla
Stan. Overlooking Stockholm Bay, it is
a great option for a macchiato and a
brioche, or a takeaway sandwich to be
enjoyed by the waterfront. Its success
has led to expansion and there are now
branches of Albert & Jack's in Fredsgatan,
Engelbrektsgatan and Drottninggatan,
but we prefer the original. After brunch,
have a mooch around the numerous
galleries that line pretty Österlanggatan.
*Skeppsbron 24, T 411 5045,*
*www.albertjacks.com*

### 13.00 Konsthantverkarna

After 55 years at its previous premises, Konsthantverkarna's boutique moved to its happening current location in the Slussen area in 2005, assuming a savvy new persona in the process. A kind of union for professional Swedish craftsmen working in glass, sculpture, ceramics, textiles, jewellery, silver, wood and leather, Konsthantverkarna comprises 93 artists who've cast off old-fashioned handiwork in favour of slick, high-quality design. The place is filled with tabletop pieces and utensils, as well as exclusive objets d'art, making this as much a gallery to go to for inspiration as it is a shop. Refuel with the set lunch amid panoramic views at the seemingly precarious Gondolen (T 641 7090), a short stroll away. *Södermalmstorg 4, T 611 0370, www.konsthantverkarna.se*

## 18.00 Fotografiska

Stockholm's first and only photography museum is located in a fantastic art nouveau building designed by Ferdinand Boberg. The old customs house, which dates from 1906, was converted into a vast museum in 2010 by two Swedish practices, AIX Architects and Guise. It shows four major photo exhibitions per year – it has headlined stars such as Annie Leibovitz, Albert Watson (above) and Robert Mapplethorpe – but this is also the place to see cutting-edge work by local photographers. Make sure you pay a visit to the well-stocked bookshop, and also check out the view across the archipelago through the large windows in the bar and restaurant, which is overseen by top Swedish chef Paul Svensson. *Stadsgårdshamnen 22, T 5090 0500, www.fotografiska.eu*

### 19.30 Lilla Baren and Riche

Jostling for space in the small but bijou Lilla Baren bar (opposite) are Stockholm's hottest party people; this isn't the place for an intimate evening à deux. Chandeliers made of upturned glasses hang over the bar, there's ornate stucco-work on the ceiling and, if you can see them, monthly exhibitions by emerging artists are hung on the walls. Arrive before 11pm to stand a chance of getting in at weekends, when DJs take to the decks. The adjoining Restaurang Riche (above), which attracts a similarly chichi crowd, is housed in an 1893 mansion, redesigned by Jonas Bohlin and furnished with his 'Tivoli' sofas. The kitchen focuses on classic dishes, which can include Toast Skagen with Kalix caviar, and Swedish fish and chips. *Birger Jarlsgatan 4, T 5450 3560, www.riche.se*

# URBAN LIFE
## CAFÉS, RESTAURANTS, BARS AND NIGHTCLUBS

The culinary scene here has evolved enormously in the past decade. Traditionally, Stockholmers entertained at home, but these days they increasingly commandeer the city itself as an extra living room. Many restaurants used to be half-empty midweek, but booking in advance is now essential (note that many places close on Sundays). True, it's not cheap, and the alcohol prices are as scary as you've heard but, in return, the quality is outstanding, menus are exciting and high-end restaurants often have wine cellars to rival those in New York or Paris. The expense, however, has fostered a trend for more casual dining – at Pubologi (Stora Nygatan 20, T 5064 0086), Stockholm's first gastro pub, it's all communal tables, draught beer, burgers and black sausages.

What hasn't changed is the Swedish penchant for coffee, cake and a good gossip. Stockholm has displayed notable prowess in keeping the corporates off the streets – the only Starbucks are at major transport hubs – to maintain a vibrant café culture. Soak it up at Konditori Valand (Surbrunnsgatan 48, T 300 476), where the teak interior (and owners) have been in place since 1954. Regarding nightlife, Stockholm is fairly conservative. Bars are quiet until the weekend, when the party goes on into the early hours and queuing is routine. Be aware that dress codes vary, from suited and booted in Östermalm to vintage and dressed down in Södermalm. *For full addresses, see Resources.*

## Bar Central

Local design studio Uglycute took this restaurant/bar's central European menu as a starting point and mixed Slavic nostalgia with modern Scandinavian interiors. Somehow the mishmash of zigzagged tiled floors, crocheted lace curtains, fibreboard panelling, brass furnishings and a tan and dark-green colour scheme seems to work. The distinctive 'Staplebar' stools were designed by Swede Lars Stensö. This is the place to come for *mittel*-European cuisine, such as the excellent Wiener schnitzel with anchovy and caper butter, and the crispy cherry strudel with cinnamon ice cream. As you'd expect, the bar has one of the city's best selections of German and Austrian wines, and Czech and German beers.
*Skånegatan 83, T 644 2420,*
*www.barcentral.se*

**Gastrologik**
This restaurant, adorned with copper, leather and wood by Malmö-based architect Jonas Lindvall, and furnished with his 'Miss Holly' chairs and 'W124' pendant lights, delivers new Nordic cuisine at its best. Young chefs Jacob Holmström and Anton Bjuhr conjure up delicacies such as fillet of deer with beetroot jus and parsnip ice cream.
*Artillerigatan 14, T 662 3060*

## Operakällaren

The direct translation may be 'opera cellar', but this is no dingy basement. Set at street level, and looking out over the water to the Royal Palace, the 1895 dining room is nothing short of a fairy tale. In 2005, Claesson Koivisto Rune gave the restaurant a facelift, which drew praise for the clever use of mirrors to showcase the exquisite ceiling, chandeliers and carved oak walls, but criticism for the choice of upholstered chairs and lights. However, there's no denying that the refurbishment placed Operakällaren firmly back on the A-list, and it remains the dining destination that (still) makes locals most proud. *Operahuset, Karl X11:s Torg, T 676 5800, www.operakallaren.se*

## KB

Short for KonstnärsBaren, or 'Artist Bar', KB is as popular today as when it opened 80 years ago. This is a classic Swedish bistro and the preferred haunt of artists, actors and hacks, and is beautifully preserved in its original shape and form; even the tables and chairs date back to 1931. The restaurant is housed in the Konstnärshuset ('Artist House'), which includes five floors of gallery space that host exhibitions throughout the year, and the restaurant itself is adorned with art and murals. In terms of the menu, we recommend the starter of four types of pickled herring – a house speciality – and the suckling veal to follow. Try to book ahead, as lunchtimes in particular get very busy.

*Smålandsgatan 7, T 679 6032, www.konstnarsbaren.se*

**Miss Voon**

The deep red interior by Thomas Sandell,
who also custom-designed the furniture,
reflects Miss Voon's trademark spiciness.
The Asian fusion menu features 15 sharing
plates, such as lobster with wasabi and
pork with *yuzukosho*, as well as sashimi.
Cool down with a Stranger in Moscow
cocktail – vodka, sake, vanilla, ginger, lime
and soda, served in an ice-cold copper cup.
*Sturegatan 22, T 5052 4470*

## PA&Co

Perched on a quiet corner in Östermalm, this die-hard diner has been serving *husmanskost* (hearty Swedish fare) to perfection for 25 years. Defying the capital's ever-changing restaurant trends, it's still a busy spot for Stockholm's fashion and media elite to see and be seen. Inside the intimate bistro, which is furnished with leather sofas, marble-topped tables and vintage chandeliers, the atmosphere is cosy and Continental. Scrawled on a chalkboard is a hardly legible menu, but those in the know simply order the regular dishes, such as beef Rydberg and PA&Co's famous Gino dessert, comprising warm fruit, white chocolate and vanilla ice cream. *Riddargatan 8, T 611 0845, www.paco.se*

## BAR

An acronym for Blasieholmens Akvarium o Restaurang, BAR is the sister restaurant of Michelin-starred Lux (T 619 0190) and is certainly the more approachable of the two. Opened in 2009, the roomy dining hall was designed by local architecture firm Koncept, which was also responsible for Story Hotel (see p024). Featuring generous windows, white-tiled walls and oak tables, BAR has an informal food-hall feel; daily specials are written on to blackboards and mirrors. Seafood is the speciality here, although there are also meat and vegetarian options. The menu changes several times a year, but will often include crispy cod with French fries or the comfort-food classic, fish and shellfish casserole.

*Blasieholmsgatan 4a, T 611 5335,*
*www.restaurangbar.se*

### Den Gyldene Freden

Dating back to 1722, Den Gyldene Freden, meaning 'Golden Peace', was named in honour of the treaty signed at Nystad that ended the Great Northern War. It is owned by the Swedish Academy, which selects the Nobel Prize for Literature; rumour has it that many a prize has been decided in the Bellman room upstairs, where the group convenes every Thursday. The middle vault (opposite) remains intact; other spaces, such as the Zorn Room (above), named after former owner and artist Anders Zorn, showcase architect Torsten Stubelius' 1922 refurbishment. The menu mixes traditional Swedish cooking with more innovative inventions. Try the meatballs served with cucumber, lingonberries and cream sauce. *Österlånggatan 51, T 249 760, www.gyldenefreden.se*

## Svartengrens

Nose-to-tail eating has been a major hit in Stockholm, with establishments championing locally produced meat and previously forgotten, slow-cooking recipes. Svartengrens takes the origins of its produce seriously, and the menu explains in detail where and under which conditions each animal was reared. Chef Göran Svartengren sends out simply prepared rib-eyes from the archipelago and sirloin from Skövde; there are also a few chicken and fish alternatives, although vegetarians will not find much joy. The understated, stylish decor of white walls and furnishings, dark stone floors, vintage chairs and big windows is casual and welcoming. Svartengrens is also famous for its drinks, many of which are made with berries picked from Swedish forests and aquavit flavoured on the premises. *Tulegatan 24, T 612 6550, www.svartengrens.se*

### Restaurang AG

It doesn't take long to figure out what AG is all about. At the entrance, large cuts of meat hang in a huge glass refrigerator, accompanied by thousands of bottles of wine. Chef Johan Jureskog and Klas Ljungquist, who together own restaurant Rolfs Kök (T 101 696), took over in 2011 and commissioned Jonas Bohlin to create the interiors of this former silver factory (hence 'AG'), which feature butcher's tiles, light fixtures from Småland, leather from Tännsjö and custom-made chairs. Meat from the region's farms, including Välnäs lamb in spring, is served alongside specialities from around the world, including Black Angus beef and Iberico Bellota; game is available in winter. The Porterhouse steak is the signature dish.
*Kronobergsgatan 37, T 4106 8100, www.restaurangag.se*

## Pontus!

Chef Pontus Frithiof is culinary royalty in Stockholm. He opened his first eaterie at 27 – after training in Paris from the age of 15 under Swedes Leif Mannerström and Erik Lallerstedt – and Pontus! arrived in 2007. Following an extensive refurb after swallowing up a neighbouring restaurant, the venue now boasts a large cocktail bar featuring plenty of Carrara marble and copper detailing, a seafood bar that claims to sell the best oysters and champagne in town, a deli, and a show kitchen and dining room (above), which has Thonet chairs and flashes of bright lime. But the standout space remains the original restaurant (overleaf), decorated with the now iconic bookshelf wallpaper, where a brasserie de luxe menu is served. *Brunnsgatan 1, T 5452 7300, www.pontusfrithiof.com*

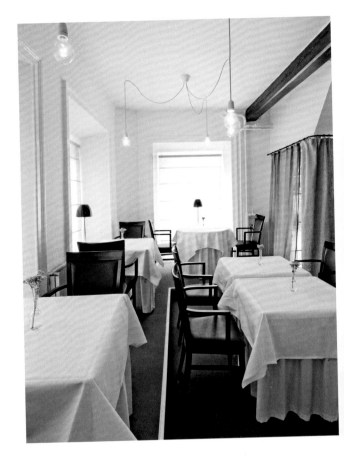

### Frantzén/Lindeberg

In 2008, chefs Bjorn Frantzén and Daniel Lindeberg opened what is quite possibly the best restaurant in town. In the same year, they enhanced the space by positioning a counter table in front of the kitchen, with enough room for four diners to observe the culinary action from the comfort of Olby-designed chairs. Otherwise, the restaurant is a modest 'at-home' setting where up to 24 people can enjoy Frantzén/Lindeberg's inventive menu, a delicate balancing of Nordic and Asian cuisine, incorporating anything from bee pollen to summer truffles and honey cress, and vegetables grown in their own organic garden. The wine list has a specific focus on labels from Burgundy, Champagne, Rhône, Alsace and Piedmont.
*Lilla Nygatan 21, T 208 580,*
*www.frantzen-lindeberg.com*

## Teatergrillen

This no-windows restaurant, complete with low lighting, red velvet booths and stone walls, comes as close to power dining, Mafia-style, as it gets in Sweden. Taking full advantage of its proximity to Dramaten (the magnificent theatre founded by King Gustav III in 1788 for Swedish dramas to be performed in their original language), the interior takes on a luxurious *Moulin Rouge* feel, with a collection of masks and costumes and a frieze depicting a stunning view over the rooftops of Paris. Ask for the corner booth (table 53), order the salt-baked entrecôte with Béarnaise, warm horseradish and pommes Pont Neuf, then head next door to aristocratic members' club Noppe Bar (T 8678 1030) to clinch the deal.
*Nybrogatan 3, T 5450 3565,*
*www.teatergrillen.se*

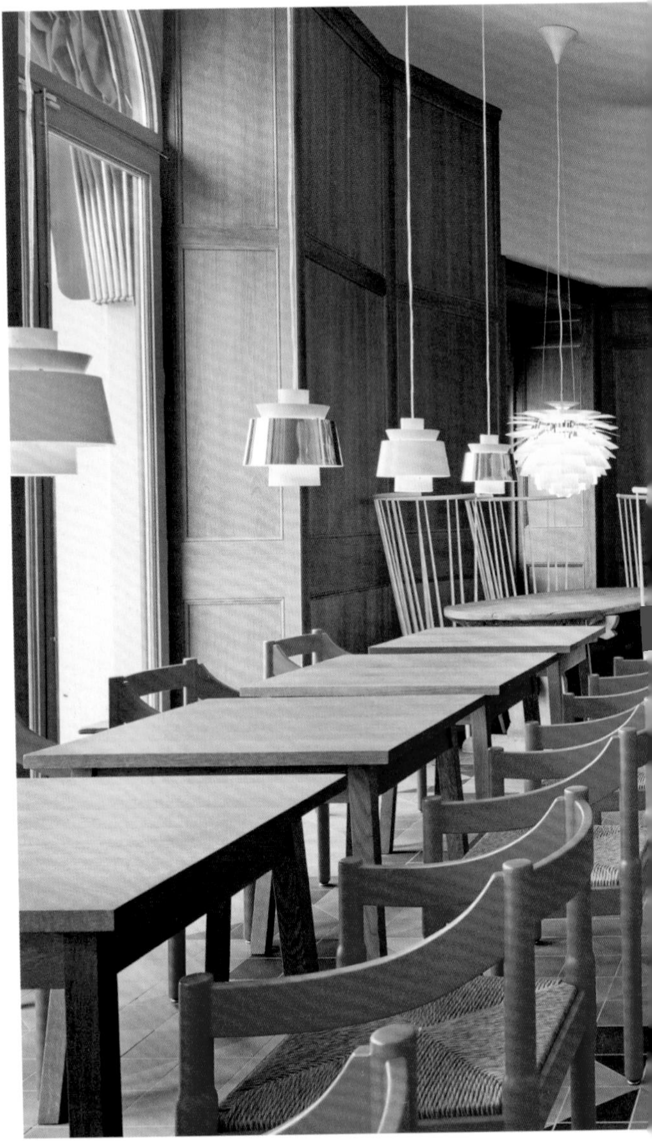

**Matbaren**
Literally the 'Food Bar', Matbaren is part
of Restaurant Mathias Dahlgren at the
Grand Hôtel (see p016). With a Michelin
star to its name – the other half of this
paradise for foodies, Matsalen (the
'Dining Room'), has two – it's a superb
venue in which to enjoy innovative and
exquisite dishes in a relaxed setting.
*Södra Blasieholmshamnen 6,*
*T 679 3584, www.mathiasdahlgren.com*

# INSIDER'S GUIDE
## SEPIDAR HOSSEINI, DESIGNER AND ILLUSTRATOR

Born to Iranian parents in Minsk and raised in Stockholm, Sepidar Hosseini's designs – from carpets to wallpaper and mosaics – are infused with global influences. She lives in Midsommarkransen, a district that grew up in the 1930s around the LM Ericsson factory, now the Konstfack art and design school. 'Every year, Stockholm feels like a new city as places and phenomena pop up all the time,' she says. 'I love its cultural richness and the nearness to water.'

Konditori Kalaskransen (Svandammsvägen 17, T 645 1588) is where Hosseini starts her ideal day, followed by a trawl of the local antiques stores. For lunch, she is a fan of the café at Färgfabriken (Lövholmsbrinken 1, T 645 3307), an art and architecture space, or Mångkulturellt Centrum Tavernan (Värdshusvägen 7, T 5317 0547), for its 'insanely good vegetarian food'. Afterwards she might catch an exhibition at Magasin 3 (Frihamnen, T 5456 8040) or Galleri Magnus Karlsson (Fredsgatan 12, T 660 4353), or look for vintage pieces at Myorna (Adolf Fredriks Kyrkogata 5-7, T 5452 0891). In the evenings, Hosseini often attends a dance performance at Moderna Dansteatern (Slupskjulsvägen 30, T 611 1456). On special occasions she'll book a table at Restaurang Landet (LM Ericssons Väg 27, T 4101 9320) or Restaurang AG (see p054), before catching a gig at Södra Teatern (Mosebacke Torg 1-3, T 5319 9490). 'Or I go to the Bodyjar club at Färgfabriken and dance all night long.'
*For full addresses, see Resources.*

# ARCHITOUR

## A GUIDE TO STOCKHOLM'S ICONIC BUILDINGS

When the Social Democratic Party implemented reforms in 1932, public housing was made Swedish architecture's main focus. The city waved goodbye to the neoclassical buildings popularised at the turn of the century by architects such as Ivar Tengbom and Gunnar Asplund in favour of stern, modern projects that embraced a functionalist aesthetic. In the coming decades, a restrictive government agenda meant that gaining planning permission for individual projects became almost impossible. Due to ambitious schemes such as the Million Homes Programme between 1965 and 1974, few architects were given scope to experiment, the exception being Peter Celsing and his 1974 Kulturhuset (see p014).

Aside from a building boom in the late 1980s in which private developers took a leading role, it wasn't until the mid-1990s, when the rapid growth of the IT industry generated demand for office space, that intriguing contemporary structures started to crop up. As architecture practices set up in the city, including White (see p010), Sandellsandberg and Tham & Videgård, and foreign firms, such as Foster + Partners and Bjarke Ingels Group, were invited to help shape the cityscape, Stockholm finally started to gain the forward-thinking landmarks it deserves. The change might be slow, but it is steady. For a superior overview of Swedish architecture, visit Arkitekturmuseet (Exercisplan 4, T 5872 7000). *For full addresses, see Resources.*

### Koppartälten

Designed by Louis-Jean Desprez for the King's Guards, and built between 1787 and 1790, the three Copper Tents are a magical addition to the already dreamlike Haga Park. Gustav III commissioned the tents as part of an attempt to build his own version of Versailles, which had apparently made a great impact on him. Unfortunately, the pavilions are all that remain of his vision, as the project was terminated by his assassination in 1792. Today, the middle structure houses a museum detailing the park's history, and the chic café located in the eastern tent, designed by Torbjörn Olsson, is an aluminium masterpiece. *Hagaparken, Solna, T 277 002, www.koppartalten.se*

## Sven-Harrys Konstmuseum

This 2011 building, financed by Swedish real-estate mogul Sven-Harry Karlsson, houses a contemporary art museum and – entrepreneurs never being ones to miss an opportunity – swanky flats. Architects Gert Wingårdh and Anna Höglund clad it in a golden alloy similar to that used for coins, interspersed with tinted windows, and the solid mass resembles a bank vault. Inside are two floors of exhibition space, a restaurant (T 5090 7830), a rooftop sculpture park and a penthouse. This space's interiors are a replica of those in Karlsson's 18th-century Lidingö mansion, and display his impressive collection of 20th-century Scandinavian art and design, including paintings by Carl Fredrik Hill. *Eastmansvägen 10-12, T 5116 0060, www.sven-harrys.se*

## Markuskyrkan

Sigurd Lewerentz's geometric, undulating, fortress-like church is tucked discreetly in a white-birch grove in Björkhagen. Built from 1956 to 1960, it's one of Lewerentz's last works, stunning in its simplicity and its considered use of materials. He requested only dark-red brick – to be left uncut – and shunned window frames or door casings to avoid disturbing the whole. The crypt-like nave receives a single shaft of light from a window high on the southern wall below the vaulted ceiling. Equally restrained and moving is Lewerentz and Gunnar Asplund's cemetery, Skogskyrkogården (T 5083 1730), constructed between 1917 and 1940. Three chapels are delicately placed within a sparse pine forest and have sweeping, open views. It is a truly cerebral landscape. *Malmövägen 51, T 5058 1501, www.svenskakyrkan.se*

**Lending Hall, Stadsbiblioteket**
Stockholm's public library is perhaps its
most internationally acclaimed structure.
Gunnar Asplund's last building to embrace
Nordic classicism (it was unveiled in 1928)
also borrows forms and ornament from
ancient Egypt. A processional stairway
leads up into the magnificent rotunda,
in which the reader is surrounded with
books on seemingly endless shelves.
*Odengatan 63, T 5083 1100*

# SHOPPING
## THE BEST RETAIL THERAPY AND WHAT TO BUY

Nordic design has undergone a renaissance in the past few years, with Sweden as the major player. Following in the footsteps of Claesson Koivisto Rune, Thomas Sandell and Jonas Bohlin are David & Martin, Monica Förster and Anna Kraitz. Even better, most of the noted showrooms are within walking distance of each other. Svenskt Tenn's flagship (Strandvägen 5, T 670 1600), and vintage furniture emporiums Modernity (see p081) and Jackson's (Sibyllegatan 53, T 665 3350), are a great introduction. Indie boutiques are also popping up – be sure to check out Strömbergs (Sibyllegatan 22, T 070 872 8275), and stylist Lotta Agaton's studio (Rådmansgatan 7, T 070 899 2998), open on Thursdays. The latest trends are on show at Designgalleriet (Odengatan 21, T 230 021).

Swedish fashion may be less renowned, but when it comes to original, quality clothes, the Stockholm high street is hard to beat. Brands like Acne (see p078) and Filippa K (Grev Turegatan 18, T 5458 8888) have made waves internationally, but are cheaper when buying in kronor. Less well-known, but equally desirable, are the elegant Rodebjer (Jakobsbergsgatan 6, T 4104 6095) and V Ave Shoe Repair (see p082). Krukmakargatan in Södermalm has several tempting diversions – among them Brandstationen (see p084) and Nitty Gritty (No 26, T 658 2440), which stocks global labels, but does so in a fanciful, fresh interior.

*For full addresses, see Resources.*

### Palmgrens

Saddlemaker and leather-worker Johannes Palmgren established his company here in 1896. Lately the heritage brand has made a comeback, thanks to its iconic leather-trimmed rattan tote (above), SEK2,595, first launched in brown in 1950 and now available in an array of bright colours. Many of Palmgrens' bags and accessories, which include everything from iPad cases to jewellery boxes, are made from organic Tärnsjö leather, and are sewn in family-run saddleries in Sweden, and in Italy and Spain. The Sibyllegatan store (T 667 9040) was refurbished in 2010 with the help of local design agency Koncept, and many of the original furnishings were kept; some of the vitrines date from the 1920s, and the life-size wooden horse, which has real hair, has been there since the start. *www.palmgrens.se*

## Hope

Designers Ann Ringstrand and Stefan
Söderberg founded Hope in 2001, and
their masculine look for women, originally
based on men's utility-wear and uniforms,
was an immediate hit. Today, there is also
a men's line. Details are a calling card of
the label – asymmetrical pockets, hidden
fastenings, contrasting fabrics, and
stitching in varying thicknesses and colour
provide both interest and functionality.
This flagship store on Norrmalmstorg
square was opened in 2011, designed
by architects Johan Lytz and Christian
Halleröd. Spray-painted white ceilings,
and exposed piping, tiled walls and
custom-made wooden cabinets evince
a well-balanced mixture of industrial
minimalism and old-fashioned pharmacy.
There is another branch at Odengatan 70.
*Smålandsgatan 14, T 4106 4123,*
*www.hope-sthlm.com*

## Asplund

Michael, Thomas and Sandra Asplund have been supplying stylish Stockholmers with clean, elegant furniture for more than two decades. Offering contemporary classics and special commissions from some of Sweden's top creatives, Asplund has launched several careers, including those of Ola Wihlborg and Stina Sandwall, and produced new ranges by old favourites such as Claesson Koivisto Rune and Thomas Sandell. It might well skirt around the experimental and conceptual aspects of modern Swedish design, but Asplund remains a testament to high-quality, functional and chic Scandinavian style.
*Sibyllegatan 31, T 662 5284, www.asplund.org*

## Byredo

This is a rare independent success in a perfume industry dominated by the big fashion houses. Founded in 2006 by Ben Gorham, the brand was soon picked up by Colette in Paris. Byredo's success is easy to understand: its selection of pure scents, some with only five core ingredients, stands out from the mass of industrially produced fragrances. The flagship store in Stockholm features a beautiful interior by designers Christian Halleröd and Johannes Svartholm, and offers the full range of intriguingly named scents, such as Mister Marvelous, winner of a Wallpaper* Design Award in 2012, alongside perfumed candles and body products. For those who can't make it to the store while in town, Byredo is also sold in Liberty in London.
*Mäster Samuelsgatan 6, T 5250 2615, www.byredo.com*

**Acne**

Launched in 1996 by Stockholm-based design firm Ambition to Create Novel Expressions, Acne jeans' signature red stitching and minimalist Scandinavian style received global attention almost overnight. Although the brand is now represented worldwide, we recommend a visit to its flagship store (pictured). *Norrmalmstorg 2, T 611 6411, www.acnestudios.com*

### Gamla Lampor

Vintage lamps and clocks obscure the walls and ceiling as you enter Gamla Lampor, which stockpiles furniture and design objects from the 1930s to the 1970s. Unusually for this part of the world, the store is completely cluttered, although there's more breathing space in the cellar, where a lovely mix of endlessly covetable items is housed, many pieces hailing from Scandinavia. We were drawn to Nils Strinning's 'String' shelving, an Ericofon cobra telephone, Poul Henningsen's 'PH Artichoke' lamp, Joe Colombo's 'Brillio' chair and much more, including a few contemporary finds by local designers such as Jonas Bohlin. Nearby are the refurbished Svenskt Tenn (see p072), Modernity (opposite) and Asplund (see p076), if you are craving cleaner lines. *Almlöfsgatan 3, T 611 9035*

## Modernity

Focusing on Scandinavian lighting, textiles, furniture, glassware, jewellery and ceramics produced between the 1930s and the 1950s, this showroom is owned not by a Swede, but by a Scotsman, Andrew Duncanson, who moved here in 1995. Modernity is famed for its collection, in particular by the grand masters such as Wegner, Mathsson, Aalto, Juhl, Jacobsen, Wirkkala and Sarpaneva, but it is the occasional limited editions by established Swedish designers, from Mats Theselius to Jonas Bohlin, that are worth fighting over. You'll also find vintage pieces from outside the region, by the likes of Gio Ponti, Marcel Breuer, Gerrit Rietveld and Fernand Léger, and a range of modern items by emerging designers such as Caroline Schlyter. *Sibyllegatan 6, T 208 025, www.modernity.se*

## V Ave Shoe Repair

Named after a historic cobblers in Goodge Street, London, V Ave Shoe Repair was founded in 2004 by Astrid Olsson and Lee Cotter and focused on delicate women's knits and jerseys. Today, it is internationally renowned as a leader in men's and women's tailoring, its experimental cuts and dramatic draping helping to establish its iconic image. In addition to its first shop in Södermalm (T 642 8055), the label opened its second outlet (above) in 2009. The store was designed by architectural firm Guise, which used the brand's style and designs as inspiration for the interiors. *Mäster Samuelsgatan 2, T 611 1640, www.vave-shoerepair.com*

### Malmstenbutiken

Carl Malmsten's wooden furniture is as Swedish as herring and aquavit. He won a 1916 competition to furnish Stadshuset, and later founded the country's carpentry school. His store on Strandvägen (T 233 380) has been operating on the ground floor of a 1904 art nouveau building for more than 70 years, and is now run by his grandson. It sells all the classics, including the 'Lilla Åland' dining chairs and colourful 'Samsas' sofas, and everything is manufactured by Swedish craftsmen. Also on sale are items by contemporary Nordic designers, and traditional handicrafts. Look out for the rag rugs (weaves of recycled materials), Gotland sheepskins and sculptural stainless steel, such as Eero Hyrkäs' Lapland-made 'JAUR' coffee pot (above), SEK1,910. *www.malmsten.se*

**Brandstationen**

Every Saturday, hip young things are to be found browsing the boutiques around Mariatorget, of which Brandstationen is an essential stop. From the concrete floor to the 5m-high ceilings, this 1902 fire station is crammed with vintage items, including furniture, kilims, oil lamps, toys, glassware and posters, and accessories such as men's watches, sunglasses and jewellery. The selection is part covetable Scandinavian chic, part kitsch, mostly from the 1950s and 1960s, with some art deco thrown in. On our visit we found an Arne Jacobsen 'Svanen' chair, Nagel candle holders, Harry Bertoia's 'Diamond' chair and a brass ASEA floor light. Other shops worth a browse on Krukmakargatan include the bookstore Papercut (T 133 574) and Our Legacy (T 668 2060), for cutting-edge Swedish menswear.
*Krukmakargatan 22, T 658 3010, www.herrjudit.se*

## Gallery Pascale

Pascale Cottard-Olsson's small but influential gallery in Östermalm exhibits contemporary design by Swedish and international names – be it furniture, ceramics, textiles, glass, illustrations or graphic design – such as Ilkka Suppanen, Thomas Sandell, Alexander Lervik, Björn Dahlström, Mats Theselius and Monica Förster. The gallery also sells its own range of unique objects in limited series. Among the many highlights are Luca Nichetto's playful, delicate 'Les Poupées' ceramic and glass vases, Claesson Koivisto Rune's asymmetric 'Eve' aluminium bracelets and Fredrik Mattson's architectonic 'Lumière' candle holders (above), SEK299. Most of the covetable items are the perfect size to fit into your suitcase.

*Humlegårdsgatan 15, T 663 6160, www.gallerypascale.com*

### Östermalms Saluhall

Generations of gourmands have visited Östermalms Saluhall since it opened in 1888 to pick up everything from bread and cheese to reindeer meat and bleak roe. One can easily spend a couple of hours ambling around beneath the glass ceilings of this market, sampling the fare and watching the locals fight for the best cuts. Visit Lisa Elmqvist (T 5534 0400), the finest stall for fish and seafood, where you can dine at the counter on the catch of the day. For meat, game and grouse, B Andersson Fågel & Vilt (T 662 5557) remains unsurpassed, Robert's Coffee (T 662 5106) grinds fresh beans for every cup it serves, and Nybroe Smørrebrød (T 662 2320) has some of the best open sandwiches in Stockholm – we recommend sampling the daily trio.
*Östermalmstorg, www.ostermalmshallen.se*

# SPORTS AND SPAS
## WORK OUT, CHILL OUT OR JUST WATCH

Considering its small population, Sweden's success in global sport is hugely impressive. Activities such as tennis, skiing, athletics, ice hockey and golf regularly produce world champions. In part, this is due to the nation's enthusiasm for keeping fit – a passion not reliant on the weather. Stockholm offers fantastic indoor facilities such as the dreamy Sturebadet (see p092), the courts at the Royal Lawn Tennis Club (see p094) and Centralbadet (Drottninggatan 88, T 5452 1300), which, although a public swimming pool, puts most other inner-city installations to shame. And as the winter landscape offers cross-country skiing, long-distance ice-skating and ice hockey just a short drive from the centre, locals never let the cold get in the way of staying active. As the Scandic saying goes: 'There's no such thing as bad weather, just bad clothes.'

In summer, the locals' determination to enjoy the few weeks of glorious sunshine means a plethora of alfresco activities. Every Stockholmer has their personal favourite bathing spot – be it the Fågelöudde beach on Lidingö, complete with water slides, diving boards and saunas, or a hidden little rock on Kastellholmen. The city's proximity to the wet stuff also means that watersports are very popular, with fishing and sailing high on the agenda. On land, bicycles are the preferred mode of transport and cyclists are well catered for, with lanes and parking bays in abundance.

*For full addresses, see Resources.*

### Yasuragi Hasseludden

This Japanese-themed spa might sacrifice cosy for all-encompassing but it is hugely popular. Architect Yoji Kasajima's organic building was commissioned by Swedish workers' union LO as a school in 1970, and was converted in 1997. The 20,000 sq m complex now includes a large indoor pool, several saunas, jacuzzis and steam rooms. There is a multitude of treatments and classes in meditation, sushi-making and more. The spa's Tokyo restaurant melds Swedish and Japanese cuisine, and the adjoining sake bar overlooks the 'garden of wandering and tranquillity', landscaped by NOD and artist Gunilla Bandolin. This stretches to the coast, comprising Swedish cherry trees, Japanese maple, mountain ash, magnolia and bamboo.
*Hamndalsvägen 6, Saltsjö-Boo,
T 747 6100, www.yasuragi.se*

**Ericsson Globe**
At 110m in diameter and 85m high, the 'giant golf ball' opened in 1989 and is still the largest spherical building in the world. Sweden's premier sporting venue holds 16,500 fans and hosts ice hockey, *innebandy* (floorball) and rock concerts. Two glass gondolas on rails snaking over the top were added in 2010 to create Stockholm's take on the London Eye.
*Globentorget 2, T 600 9100*

### Sturebadet

The luxurious Sturebadet baths, gym and spa complex was founded in 1885. Its distinctive facade was modelled on a Renaissance palace in Venice, and has long been at the centre of Stockholm life. Its swimming pool (right), added in 1902, has a Jugendstil interior designed by Hjalmar Molin, who incorporated Old Norse and Moorish elements. A fire razed the complex in 1985 but it was faithfully rebuilt over a period of four years based on original photographs. A peaceful oasis, Sturebadet is members-only but a limited number of guest day passes are available (from SEK495). There are more than 50 treatments to indulge in; the Classic Spa includes a full Swedish body massage, pedicure and facial. The restaurant, Curman (T 611 8090), survived the fire and serves a legendary breakfast.
*Sturegallerian 36, T 5450 1500,*
*www.sturebadet.se*

**Kungliga Tennishallen**
The illustrious Royal Lawn Tennis Club
was designed by top Swedish architect
Sture Frölén in a functionalist style and
opened mid-war in 1943. It has stood
the test of time, and the Stockholm Open
is still held here every October. Follow
in the footsteps of local hero Björn Borg
and take to one of the 15 indoor hard
courts or six outdoor clay surfaces.
*Lidingövägen 75, T 459 1500, www.kltk.se*

# ESCAPES

**WHERE TO GO IF YOU WANT TO LEAVE TOWN**

For all of Stockholm's attempts to come across as metropolitan, you just know that she's a country girl at heart. The city is in such easy reach of so many places of pristine natural beauty that it would be criminal not to take advantage. Most spectacular is the vast and unique fan-shaped archipelago that stretches out more than 100km from Saltsjön into a magical island world. Known as the 'urban wilderness', the area consists of more than 30,000 islands, of which only a few hundred are inhabited, and is home to some of the best hotels and restaurants in Scandinavia.

Extended daylight hours mean early May to late August are the peak times to head out to the archipelago, but winter can offer just as spectacular scenery, when ice-skating and warming up in front of cosy fires are high on the agenda. Bear in mind that only the larger establishments, such as Utö Värdshus (Gruvbryggan, T 5042 0300) and Seglarhotell (opposite), are open all year round. In summer, however, the choice is much greater – perhaps try lunch at Fjäderholmarnas Krog (Stora Fjäderholmen, T 718 3355). All are easily reached on ferries that depart from Strömkajen, Strandvägen and Slussen respectively; the more adventurous can hire their own speedboat or yacht. Alternatively, for something a little more extreme, the north of Sweden has some of the most challenging and well-maintained ski slopes (see p098) in Europe. *For full addresses, see Resources.*

### Sandhamn

You may recognise the name from the Stieg Larsson trilogy and, yes, it actually exists. Accessible only by boat or ferry, this island comes alive from April until September, when the yachting season gets underway on the Swedish east coast, and is a must for sailing enthusiasts. Most notably, it's the finishing line for the Round Gotland ÅF Offshore Race, one of the largest of its kind in the world. But you don't need sea legs to enjoy the island; there are a number of spectacular sandy beaches – Trouville, a 15-minute walk from the harbour, is one of the best. Seglarhotell (T 5745 0400) is open year round and has a great spa and restaurant (above; T 5745 0421), which has its own smoke house and is set within the former Royal Sw edish Yacht Club, which dates from 1897. *www.sandhamn.com*

## Åre

There are many ski resorts in the north of Sweden, but Åre (pronounced awe-re), a 75-minute flight then an hour's drive from Stockholm, is the most sophisticated choice. In peak season (December to April), the slopes, après-ski bars and restaurants fill up with the incredibly fresh-faced, healthy looking Swedish glitterati. It also hosts one of the largest concert stages in the mountains, where the country's hippest musicians perform. Åre has been dubbed the St Moritz of the north, but this is misleading – for all its superb eateries and hostelries, it is a charming, laidback town. It is similarly glorious in summer, when it becomes a mountain-bikers' paradise. Stay at the Diplomat Åregården (T 06 471 7900), a 1920s National Romantic pile turned boutique hotel with views over the lake.

### Bomans Hotel, Trosa

One hour south of Stockholm lies the quaint coastal village of Trosa, where pastel-coloured wooden houses line the banks of the river, and fantastic seafood restaurants, cafés and galleries are scattered around the marina. This is also where you will find the eccentric Bomans Hotel. All 45 rooms are individually decorated with items that the owners have acquired over the years, mixed in with modern design pieces from Svenskt Tenn, Fritz Hansen, Philippe Starck and Ikea. We recommend you book one of the larger rooms in the band of numbers 60-75, such as Suite 60, La Dolce Vita, where a larger-than-life photo of Anita Ekberg bathing in the Trevi Fountain serves as a headboard. *Östra Hamnplan, T 1565 2500, www.bomans.se*

**Clarion Hotel Post, Gothenburg**
Architects Semrén & Månsson and interior
designer Anemone Wille Våge have turned
Gothenburg's 1925 post office, designed
in neoclassical style by Ernst Torulf, into
a sleek hotel clad in slate and copper.
Historical features, notably the Post Hall,
have been preserved; the reception desk
is fashioned from Orrefors crystal, and
B&B Italia has furnished the 500 rooms,
such as the Standard (above) and Deluxe
(opposite), with custom-made pieces and
classics from Naoto Fukasawa and Patricia
Urquiola. There's a spa, a roof terrace and
pool, and a modern take on Swedish food
in Norda Bar & Grill, helmed by chef Marcus
Samuelsson. Three to four hours by train
from Stockholm, Gothenburg is enjoying
a creative renaissance, with much of the
action centring on the reclaimed dockland
warehouses of Klippan and Röda Sten.
*Drottningtorget 10, T 03 161 9000,*
*www.clarionpost.se*

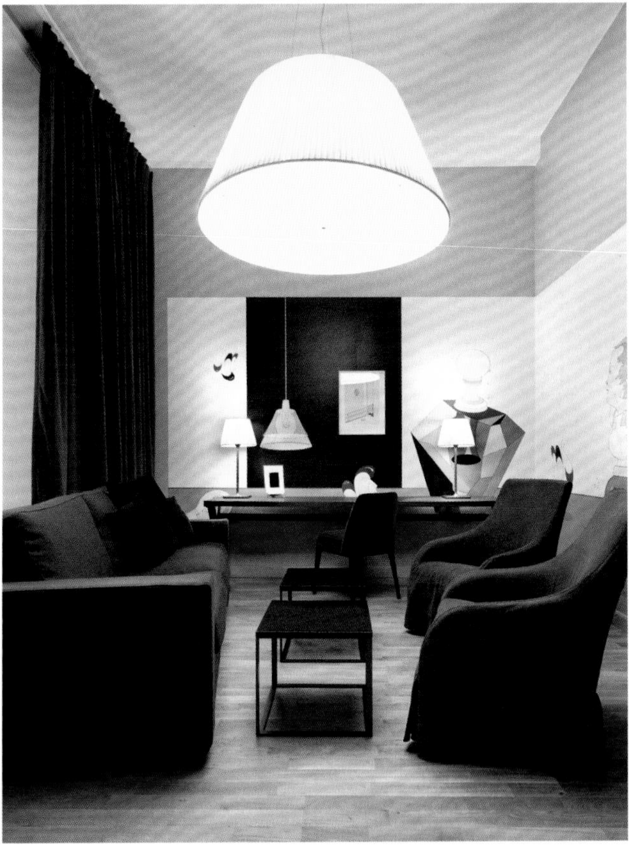

### Saltsjöbadens Friluftsbad

This bathing house, designed by Elis Kjellin and Torben Grut and completed in 1925, is a big draw for city folk wanting to escape the summer heat. Many such wooden mini-resorts lined Sweden's east coast but have now mostly been torn down. A similar fate threatened Saltsjöbaden's but after concerted protest it was renovated back to its former glory in 2006. There's a sun deck, jump towers, saunas, a restaurant and separate areas for men and women, between which is a small beach. The Saltsjöbanan train departs from Slussen and takes 30 minutes – you can't miss it, it's bright blue. If you want to stay overnight, the *only* address in town is the renovated Grand Hotel (T 5061 7000), designed in a Monte Carlo style by Erik Josephson and opened in 1893 with the idea of creating a Swedish Riviera.
*Torben Gruts Väg 8, Saltsjöbaden, T 717 0552, www.saltisbadet.se*

# NOTES

**SKETCHES AND MEMOS**

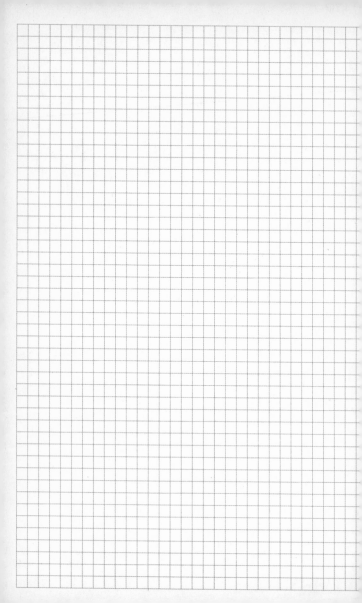

# RESOURCES
## CITY GUIDE DIRECTORY

# HOTELS
## ADDRESSES AND ROOM RATES

**Berns** 016
Room rates:
double, from SEK1,650
*Näckströmsgatan 8*
*T 5663 2200*
*www.berns.se*

**Bomans Hotel** 099
Room rates:
double, from SEK1,750;
La Dolce Vita Suite 60, from SEK2,900
*Östra Hamnplan*
*Trosa*
*T 1565 2500*
*www.bomans.se*

**Clarion Hotel** 016
Room rates:
double, from SEK1,070
*Ringvägen 98*
*T 462 1000*
*www.clarionstockholm.com*

**Clarion Hotel Post** 100
Room rates:
double, from SEK160;
Standard, SEK1,880;
Deluxe, SEK2,780
*Drottningtorget 10*
*Gothenburg*
*T 03 161 9000*
*www.clarionpost.se*

**Clarion Hotel Sign** 017
Room rates:
double, from SEK1,270;
Superior Room 1005, SEK1,470;
Suite 601, from SEK2,970
*Östra Järnvägsgatan 35*
*T 676 9800*
*www.clarionsign.com*

**Diplomat Åregården** 098
Room rates:
double, from SEK1,495
*Åre Torg*
*T 06 471 7900*
*www.diplomathotel.com*

**Hotel Esplanade** 028
Room rates:
double, SEK1,695;
Room 14, SEK1,895
*Strandvägen 7a*
*T 663 0740*
*www.hotelesplanade.se*

**Ett Hem** 018
Room rates:
double, from SEK3,800;
Suite 1, from SEK 7,500
*Sköldungagatan 2*
*T 200 590*
*www.etthemstockholm.se*

**Gåshaga Sealodge** 026
Room rates:
double, SEK1,395
*Värdshusvägen 14-16*
*Lidingö*
*T 601 3400*
*www.gashaga.nu*

**Grand Hôtel** 016
Room rates:
double, SEK2,700
*Södra Blasieholmshamnen 8*
*T 679 3500*
*www.grandhotel.se*

**Grand Hotel Saltsjöbaden** 103
Room rates:
double, SEK1,300
*Hotell Vägen 1*
*Saltjöbaden*
*T 5061 7000*
*www.grandsaltsjobaden.se*

**Lydmar Hotel** 020
  Room rates:
  double, from SEK3,200;
  X-Large Room, SEK12,500
  *Södra Blasieholmshamnen 2*
  *T 223 160*
  *www.lydmar.com*
**Nobis Hotel** 022
  Room rates:
  double, from SEK2,190;
  Deluxe 467, SEK3,590;
  Nobis Suite, SEK25,000
  *Norrmalmstorg 2-4*
  *T 614 1000*
  *www.nobishotel.se*
**Seglarhotell** 097
  Room rates:
  double, SEK2,390
  *Riddargatan 6*
  *Sandhamn*
  *T 5745 0400*
  *www.sandhamn.com*
**Hotel Skeppsholmen** 030
  Room rates:
  double, from SEK1,955;
  Room 254, from SEK2,895
  *Gröna Gången 1*
  *T 407 2350*
  *www.hotelskeppsholmen.se*
**Story Hotel** 024
  Room rates:
  double, from SEK1,790;
  Super Squeeze, SEK1,190;
  Lily Dam Suite, SEK3,190
  *Riddargatan 6*
  *T 5450 3940*
  *www.storyhotels.com*

## WALLPAPER* CITY GUIDES

**Executive Editor**
Rachael Moloney

**Editor**
Jeremy Case
**Authors**
Roberta Ellingsen Holm
Elna Nykänen Andersson

**Art Director**
Loran Stosskopf
**Art Editor**
Eriko Shimazaki
**Designer**
Mayumi Hashimoto
**Map Illustrator**
Russell Bell

**Photography Editor**
Sophie Corben
**Acting Photography Editor**
Anika Burgess
**Photography Assistant**
Nabil Butt

**Chief Sub-Editor**
Nick Mee
**Sub-Editor**
Marie Cleland Knowles

**Editorial Assistant**
Emma Harrison

**Wallpaper* Group**
**Editor-in-Chief**
Tony Chambers
**Publishing Director**
Gord Ray
**Managing Editor**
Jessica Diamond
**Acting Managing Editor**
Oliver Adamson

**Interns**
Kate Cregan
Carmen de Baets
Lillian He
Despina Rangou
Hye-Young Yune

First published 2006
Second edition (revised and updated) 2010
Third edition (revised and updated) 2011
Fourth edition (revised and updated) 2012
Reprinted 2013

All prices are correct at the time of going to press, but are subject to change.

Printed in China

## PHAIDON

**Phaidon Press Limited**
Regent's Wharf
All Saints Street
London N1 9PA

**Phaidon Press Inc**
180 Varick Street
New York, NY 10014

Phaidon® is a registered trademark of Phaidon Press Limited

www.phaidon.com

A CIP Catalogue record for this book is available from the British Library.

ISBN 978 0 7148 6638 3

# PHOTOGRAPHERS

**Sören Andersson**
Ericsson Globe,
pp090-091

**Charlie Bennet**
Ett Hem, p018, p019
Lilla Baren, p038
Riche, p039
Bar Central, p041
Gastrologik, pp042-043
Miss Voon, pp046-047
Svartengrens, pp052-053
Sepidar Hosseini, p063
Markuskyrkan,
p068, p069
Hope, pp074-075
Brandstationen,
pp084-085
Gallery Pascale, p086

**Marianne Boströ**
Kaknästornet, p012

**Peter Guenzel**
Kulturhuset, pp014-015
Koppartälten, p065
Stadsbiblioteket,
pp070-071
Asplund, p076

**Wojtek Gurak**
Stockholm Waterfront,
pp010-011

**Helena Karlsson**
Eero Hyrkäs
coffee pot, p083

**Kersti Lilja**
Saltsjöbadens Friluftsbad,
pp102-103

**Åke E:son Lindman**
Matbaren, pp060-061
Modernity, p081

**Michael McLain**
Teatergrillen, p059

**Peartree Digital**
Palmgrens rattan
bag, p073

**Christoffer Rudquist**
Stockholm city view,
inside front cover
Wenner-Gren Centre, p013
Clarion Hotel Sign, p017
Nobis Hotel, p022, p023
Story Hotel, p024, p025
Hotel Esplanade,
p028, p029
Albert & Jack's, pp034-035
Fotografiska, p037
KB, p045
PA&Co, p048
BAR, p049
Den Gyldene
Freden, p050, p051

Restaurang AG, p054
Pontus!, p055, pp056-057
Frantzén/Lindeberg, p058
Byredo, p077
Gamla Lampor, p080
Östermalms Saluhall, p087
Kungliga Tennishallen,
pp094-095

**Tord-Rickard
Söderström**
Sven-Harrys
Konstmuseum, pp066-067

**Henrik Trygg**
Djurgården, p033

**Gabriella Wachtmeister**
Gåshaga Sealodge,
pp026-027
Konsthantverkarna, p036

# STOCKHOLM
## A COLOUR-CODED GUIDE TO THE CITY'S HOT 'HOODS

### ÖSTERMALM
The chicest part of Stockholm, its avenues are lined with swanky stores and grand houses

### SKEPPSHOLMEN
Museum Island has all the culture you could desire, from art to architecture and design

### NORRMALM
The financial centre is a hubbub of offices, high-street stores, eateries and one-off cafés

### SÖDERMALM
Now a slightly left-field district with plenty of interesting retail and hip bars to explore

### VASASTADEN
Laidback and residential, this area has an emerging neighbourhood restaurant scene

### GAMLA STAN
Tourists visit the Old Town for its Royal Palace, cobbled streets and medieval townhouses

### KUNGSHOLMEN
This district is gentrifying as factories are split into lofts, and delis and bistros arrive

### DJURGÅRDEN
Stockholm's green lung is crisscrossed by woodland trails and is great for a summer dip

For a full description of each neighbourhood, see the Introduction.
Featured venues are colour-coded, according to the district in which they are located.